LIFE
IS
ACTION

BY
TERRY DAVIS

CONTENTS

INTRODUCTION

Do you ever wake up crying because you don't know where you fit in the world? Because you didn't know even why you're here? Most of what happens in life is not explained. We're just told that this is how it is, so deal with it. If only we were given more evidence on why we were created than instructions on what to do after we are created!

Whether it's because of a "Big Bang" or Adam and Eve, we are here. If you're reading these words or if you're listening to someone else read them to you, you are alive—regardless of whether you're a man or a woman, an atheist or a believer, or a Christian or a non-Christian. None of us will be able to escape life without the final destination of death, so while we're here, we might as well live out our purpose.

With that being said, we'll have many challenges that will test our faith, our families, and our finances. Some days, we will ask for prayers not to wake up, and other days we'll ask for prayers of abundance of joy. The following words are intended to inspire us to live, to love, to learn, and to strip away the lies, labels, and layers that prevent us from doing those things. — *T. Davis*

ABOUT THE AUTHOR

Terry Davis served 4 years in the United States Navy and for 8 years in the Navy Reserve. Subsequently, for more than 16 years, Terry has worked in Tennessee in the mental health field with state custody foster children. The children, who lived in a mental-health hospital for durations of 6 months to 2 years, have ranged in age from 5 to 18 years old.

After working with thousands of kids and adults, Terry realized that most cases shared a common factor: how people viewed themselves. The messages of doubt that comprised their self-talk were loud and strong. When he facilitated or became a part of the therapy groups, he noted that the individuals felt less negative after telling their stories to other people who had similar experiences and feelings. He recognized that when the group delved into the core issues, there were some basic steps that could be taken to change the negative viewpoints. That realization inspired Terry to write a book that a depressed inner-city 10-year-old and a depressed 50-year-old suburban physician could read and feel better—if only for a day.

CHAPTER 1

THE LIES

- You are dumb

- You are stupid

- You are drunk

- You are a druggie

- You are a bum

- You are a failure

- You never will never graduate

- You never will own a business

- You never will be a good son

- You never will be a good daughter

- Nobody wants you

- Nobody loves you

- You never will get married

- You never will be a good mother

- You never will be a good father

Imagine someone recording those phrases and playing them back to you every day. After a while, it will be hard not to believe those negative words! We're not inborn with a negative attitude. Our first teacher in life is our environment, which we don't get to choose before birth but which will affect us for the rest of our lives. Some people will be raised in environments that will be worse than others. Some people will be able to change the negatives into positives. Some people simply will exist but not live. Some people will keep all their dreams hidden inside. Some people will live for others.

Our environment has a lot to do with our outlook—with what we see, what we feel, what we think, and how we react. All of our attitudes and actions tie back to our innate fight-or-flight response. If we perceive that we're in danger, our bodies activate our adrenal glands and our cardiovascular systems. If this happens too often, our immune systems become depleted and weakened—and our health is at risk.

We must alert ourselves when we are importing negative information into our souls. This is a very important step toward loving ourselves. We're our own best teachers. If we continue to echo negative words and phrases, then we're as guilty as the people who belittled us in the first place. Sometimes, though, those negative voices won't be quiet; they just keep repeating themselves in our minds.

Often, we try to silence the words by overindulging in food, alcohol, drugs, and sex. Those activities may help temporarily, but the words only come back stronger and louder. We end up believing them so that we won't have to continue to fight them. As with any difficult challenge, we must love ourselves first and learn from our experiences in order to continue to live our best lives.

Don't worry about anything; instead, pray about

everything. Tell God what you need, and thank him for all he has done. Then you will experience God's peace, which exceeds anything we can understand. His peace will guard your hearts and minds as you live in Christ Jesus. (Philippians 4:6 & 7; NLT)

CHAPTER 2

THE LAYERS

- I wear a mask well! *I hide the pain and present myself as if everything is good, although I often feel bad.*

- I was told not to cry, so I didn't. *But I feel so worried and sad.*

- I was told not to express my emotions, so I didn't. *But I feel so anxious and angry.*

- I was told not to dream, so I didn't. *But I feel so hopeless and fearful.*

We must love ourselves enough to be able to take our masks off. We carry tons and tons of emotions for years. Nobody knows how we really feel because we have trained ourselves so well to wear the mask. Not until we've lost it all. Not until we've been in jail. Or have used drugs. Or have been divorced. Not until we want to commit suicide. Not until we face off with our egos, our perception of ourselves.

We must refuse to wear that mask again. We must accept who we were born to be. It's okay to be weak some days. It's okay to cry some days. It's okay to worry some days. It's okay to be anxious some days. It's okay to be angry some days. What matters is how we act when we are feeling one of those emotions. What we shouldn't do is beat ourselves up and resort to wearing the mask.

What should we do when we feel weak, sad, bothered, upset or mad? We should accept that we are human. We should ask for help and guidance. We should tune out the voices of guilt. We should learn from the negative circumstances and grow from the pain. In other words, we must be our own first responders in order to save our souls.

Think about this! Instead of wearing that mask, we must chase our dreams. Our dream to help others--Our dream to keep our family together--Our dream to go to school-- Our dream to start a business. And to do those things, we must take off our masks and love ourselves. We must release the natural positive feelings that dopamine and serotonin produce. This isn't easy to do—and it must be done every day. But we can do it by engaging in hobbies, by taking steps to reach our goals, by developing good eating habits, and by exercising and practicing deep breathing.

> But the LORD said to Samuel: "Do not look at his appearance or at the height of his stature, because I have rejected him; for God sees not as man sees, for man looks at the outward appearance, but the LORD looks at the heart. (1 Samuel 16:7; Verse Concepts)

ALSO

> But let it be the hidden person of the heart, with the

imperishable quality of a gentle and quiet spirit, which is precious in the sight of God. (1 Peter 3:4; Verse Concepts)

CHAPTER 3

THE LABELS

As I was writing the first three parts of this book, I was sitting in my hotel room. I had a sheet of paper and a few ideas. The television was on. I'm always in multitask mode, and, for some reason, I started changing channels. I stopped on TBN, where a familiar pastor was speaking. I don't remember his name, but he was a young pastor and I had seen him on YouTube a few times. Even though he had very updated messages, they were definitely connected to the Bible. The pastor had a ruler in his hand. I thought that was kind of weird but interesting, so it did its job by holding my attention. In fact, it made me turn up the volume.

Wow! Lo and behold, his sermon was on labels—or as he said, how we size people up to figure out how we will treat them. The message was so true, and it was delivered in a unique way. I thank God for that jewel! The pastor explained that when we introduce ourselves to people or when people ask you what kind of work you do, what they really are doing is measuring how they will treat you. I never could have articulated it as clearly as he did.

I do believe that people chase labels versus chasing their purpose. As I think back, I remember how, when I was a child, my parents talked to doctors, pastors, teachers, politicians, and anyone in a role superior to them. The superiority of others could be based on education, financial class, or social standing. Whatever the reason, my parents were liberal with the use of "Yes, sir" and "Yes, ma'am." I'm not discrediting the hard work or success of the people my parents were talking to. I just want to point out how we are trained early in life to make such distinctions.

What is modeled for us is likely what we will remodel when we are older. Something about that bothered me deeply when I was a kid, but at that young age, I didn't know why. I did feel that I might never get any respect unless I had one of the valued labels—labels that seemed so important when it came to providing services to other people in such helpful ways.

But there was such a contrast between those important and effective individuals and the amount of poverty present in my upbringing. Knowing that homeless people were living in the woods near my neighborhood kept me wondering. Who will help them? Who will check on them? Are they not important because they are homeless? Well, they're labeled as unimportant! We don't know their stories. We don't know their dreams. Maybe they once had respected labels but fell on hard times. Maybe they need a hand up—not just temporary food and shelter, but a way to continue to take care of themselves.

I have worked a variety of jobs during the past few decades. I was so amazed that, in my experience, what I saw as a kid was even more prevalent in the workplace, so my natural rebellious peaceful solution was to make sure that I loved the least popular, least important person in the building. For example, I made sure that, in front of other employees, I picked up paper or trash. And the janitor or housekeeper was approaching the door, I made sure that I held that door open for them, just as if the CEO of the company or another "important" person. Coworkers asked me why I did that for someone in such a "low" position. Why was I doing their job? Yet these same coworkers would jump up to act like they were working hard or being helpful when the CEO or someone else they viewed as important was present.

> *For in the same way you judge others, you will be judged, and with the measure you use, it will be measured to you. (Matthew 7:2; NIV)*

ALSO

> *Remind the people to be subject to rulers and*

authorities, to be obedient, to be ready to do whatever is good, to slander no one, to be peaceable and considerate, and always be gentle toward everyone. At one time we too were foolish, disobedient, deceived and enslaved by all kinds of passions and pleasures. We lived in malice and envy, being hated and hating one another. (Titus 3:1-4; NIV)

CHAPTER 4

LOVE

Love is one of the most powerful four-letter words that we have. "Love" has so many meanings for so many different people. The word is usually used in a compassionate way, from one person to another. That's the traditional way. It's the way the word is used from when we're very young. But as we grow and learn through many life lessons, we often forget to say "I love you" to the most important person in the world—ourselves!

Take a few minutes and think about how many times you've told others outside of your family and friends that you love them. Now think about how many times you've told yourself the same thing. It's such an important thing to tell yourself— and not just when your life is going well. It's so important—

maybe even more so—when you're feeling low or are in pain.

How we see ourselves and what we say to ourselves in private is how we show ourselves to other people. How we treat ourselves is how we allow others to treat us. Love is not just a word. Love starts within and shines a light on our actions. Love is being sympathetic to and being kind to others. Love is Action!

Doing random acts of kindness, for example, is one of the best demonstrations of love. For example, open a door, let someone go ahead of you in line, and Smile; You get the idea! Doing something for a stranger, without expecting something in return, will brighten someone else's day and will make you feel good.

Volunteering is another act of kindness that has beneficial results or other people but also can help with your own feelings of depression. I'm not saying that volunteering will cure depression, but helping others will balance your own emotional ups and downs. And volunteering may change someone else's life forever. So, help out at a soup kitchen. Donate some time to an animal shelter. Lead a neighborhood cleanup program. Do after-school tutoring. Mentor kids at church by providing help with reading, giving music lessons, or teaching baking or jewelry-making. The options are endless! And the opportunities to show love are priceless— yet, they cost nothing.

Love is patient, love is kind. It does not envy, it does not boast, it is not proud. It does not dishonor others, it is not self-seeking, it is not easily angered, it keeps no record of wrongs. (I Corinthians 13:4-5; NIV)

ALSO

Let love and faithfulness never leave you; bind them around your neck, write them on the tablet of your heart. Then you will win favor and a good name in the sight of God and man. (Proverbs 3:3-4; NIV)

CHAPTER 5

LIVING

According to scientists, in order for something to be classified as living, the organism must be made of cells, grow and develop, use energy, reproduce, respond to its environment, and adapt. With that being said, we must try to stop just surviving but really try to enjoy being alive. Easier said than done, I know!

The first step to any change or shift in mindset starts with self-awareness. We don't get to pick our biological parents, but we each have a dream that we want to live. With so many distractions and enticements competing for our attention, we must really work to live the dream we desire. Living the dream is not a question of believing that financial success will make you happy. Living the dream is what you do with that success.

Not exploring all aspects of our amazing planet, possibly leads to the most devastating self-imposed unhappiness. Nature itself is so self-soothing because of the beauty that the Creator gave us for our enjoyment. The soothing sounds of the oceans. The awe-inspiring dignity of the mountains. Walks in the woods. You don't have to take a trip to a faraway place. Trips to London, Paris, Rome are glamorous, and visits to Hawaii and the Bahamas are eye-opening. Traveling to such places is amazing and worth doing but usually is not possible. But having a picnic in a local park or visiting a local museum, taking a two-hour trip to an art festival or story-telling event, or making a two-day trip to a national park is more doable.

It's important, especially for kids, to see what's within a two-mile radius of their immediate neighborhood. In most cities, local parks, lakes, and rivers are available for sightseeing and exploration. Local museums may have special-discount— and even free—days. Libraries have updated technology that allows us to extend our imaginations beyond our physical, social, and educational limits. It's okay to live our childhood dreams, even if we're already adults. It's okay to do what we always wanted to do but didn't have the chance to do as kids. Living is more about enjoying the ability to exist in this very complicated but amazing world.

The thief comes only to steal and kill and destroy; I have come that they may have life, and have it to full. (John 10:1; NIV)

ALSO

For I know the plans that I have for you, declares the Lord, plans for prospering you and not for evil, to give you a future and a hope. (Jeremiah 29:11)

CHAPTER 6

LEARNING

Learning probably is the most used but also the most intimidating word in our vocabulary. Starting in our babyhood, other people have told us what we have to learn. From crawling we are expected to learn to walk, and sometimes by a certain age. *Learning* is drilled into us as parents, teachers, and others tell us the skills and information we're supposed to acquire and when we're supposed to acquire them.

We must consider, however, that there are different levels for learning for each human being. We must remember that every individual requires a different amount of time to achieve each level of learning. And we must take into account learning styles. Some people are experiential and others are conceptual. Still others are a combination of both.

With learning, it's so important to find out early what your learning style is. A standardized educational system sometimes makes that difficult. But it's important for adults to challenge kids by determining their strengths and weaknesses and using different techniques as part of the learning. For adults, then, the challenge is to approach learning as an opportunity to find new ways to teach rather than as a burden to impart something new.

To learn new information or a new skill takes a lot of courage. To absorb new information or achieve a new skill takes discipline and motivation. The more we learn, the more powerful and knowledgeable we become. One of the best ways to learn something new is to find another person or a group that shares your interest. In that way, you can hold each other accountable as well as encourage each other. Art, music, sewing, photography, fitness, and woodworking are only a few options. Choose an activity that has both physical and mental aspects. And try to choose a low-cost activity. Paying for the activity is likely to give you a greater need to be successful but will not make you feel embarrassed if you don't finish the program or course. The goal is to start, enjoy, and finish. We're never too old or too young to learn. We just have to have the desire and inspiration to want to have something to give away to others.

> *Teach me to do your will, for you are my God; may your good Spirit lead me on level ground. (Psalm 143:10; NIV)*

ALSO

> *The things you have learned and received and heard and seen in me, practice these things, and the God of peace will be with you. (Philippians 4:9; NIV)*

FINAL WORDS OF ADVICE

LEVERAGE STRESS

- Laugh more

- Smile at other people

- Meditate

- Pray

- Challenge yourself with new things

- Adopt a pet

- Breathe deeply (Deep breathing is another calming skill that you can use when you're in a stressful situation and need to calm down.)

- Cry (Instead of avoiding or pushing down emotions, work through them by having a good cry.)

PRACTICE GOOD SCOPING SKILLS

- Spend time on your hobbies

- Engage in spirituality

- Take time for yourself

- Engage in physical activity or exercise

- Read

- Practice healthy eating habits

- Learn your triggers (If you know what triggers your depression, you avoid them and learn how to better cope when those situations arise.)

Made in the USA
Columbia, SC
25 April 2024

34901872R00017